On the Move

FIRST EDITION

Series Editor Deborah Lock; **Designer** Sara Nunan; **US Editor** John Searcy;
Managing Art Editor Rachael Foster; **Pre-Production Producer** Nadine King; **Producer** Sara Hu;
DTP Designer Ben Hung; **Jacket Designer** Mary Sandberg;
Reading Consultant Linda Gambrell, PhD

THIS EDITION

Editorial Management by Oriel Square
Produced for DK by WonderLab Group LLC
Jennifer Emmett, Erica Green, Kate Hale, *Founders*

Editors Grace Hill Smith, Libby Romero, Michaela Weglinski;
Photography Editors Kelley Miller, Annette Kiesow, Nicole DiMella;
Managing Editor Rachel Houghton; **Designers** Project Design Company; **Researcher** Michelle Harris;
Copy Editor Lori Merritt; **Indexer** Connie Binder; **Proofreader** Larry Shea;
Reading Specialist Dr. Jennifer Albro; **Curriculum Specialist** Elaine Larson

Published in the United States by DK Publishing
1745 Broadway, 20th Floor, New York, NY 10019

Copyright © 2023 Dorling Kindersley Limited
DK, a Division of Penguin Random House LLC
22 23 24 25 26 10 9 8 7 6 5 4 3 2 1
001-333854-May/2023

All rights reserved.
Without limiting the rights under the copyright reserved above, no part of this publication may be reproduced, stored in or introduced into a retrieval system, or transmitted, in any form, or by any means (electronic, mechanical, photocopying, recording, or otherwise), without the prior written permission of the copyright owner.
Published in Great Britain by Dorling Kindersley Limited

A catalog record for this book
is available from the Library of Congress.
HB ISBN: 978-0-7440-7096-5
PB ISBN: 978-0-7440-7097-2

DK books are available at special discounts when purchased in bulk for sales promotions, premiums, fundraising, or educational use. For details, contact: DK Publishing Special Markets,
1745 Broadway, 20th Floor, New York, NY 10019
SpecialSales@dk.com

Printed and bound in China

The publisher would like to thank the following for their kind permission to reproduce their images:
a=above; c=center; b=below; l=left; r=right; t=top; b/g=background

Alamy Stock Photo: Abaca Press / Pierre Barlier 29, Joern Sackermann 6-7, Colin Underhill 19t;
Dreamstime.com: Dezzor 7cb, Monkey Business Images 30tl; **Shutterstock.com:** aappp 4-5, K.Sorokin 30cla, Monkey Business Images 16, Spotmatik Ltd 17

Cover images: *Front:* **Dreamstime.com:** Alexander Nikiforov / Steffus b; **Shutterstock.com:** RTimages tr

All other images © Dorling Kindersley
For more information see: www.dkimages.com

For the curious
www.dk.com

On the Move

Linda Esposito

Contents

- **6**   Moving Around
- **8**   Cars
- **10**   Trucks
- **12**   Trains
- **14**   Tractors
- **16**   Bicycles
- **18**   Buses

20 Airplanes
22 Hot-Air Balloons
24 Helicopters
26 Boats
28 Space Shuttles
30 Glossary
31 Index
32 Quiz

Moving Around

There are many ways to travel.

Cars

Cars go on the roads.
Vroom!

windshield

headlight

Trucks

Trucks rumble along the highway. They carry heavy loads.

trailer

Trains

Trains move fast along the railroad tracks. They zoom by.

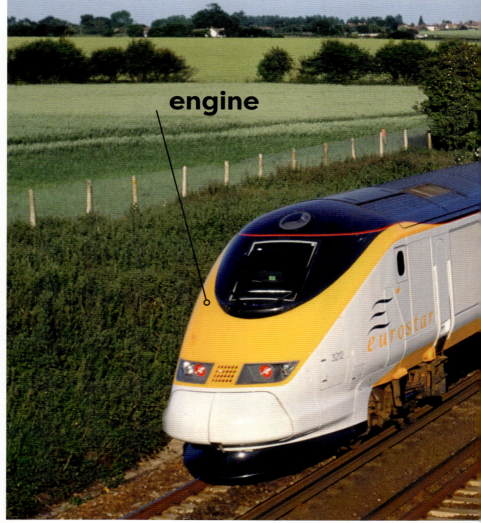

engine

Tractors

Tractors drive on farms. They go up and down the fields.

cab

tractor mower

wheel

15

Bicycles

Bicycles go along the paths. Their wheels go round and round.

helmet

wheel

Buses

Buses go along
the streets.
People get on and off.

windshield wiper

light

wing

Airplanes

Airplanes fly in the sky. Off they go.

engine

Hot-Air Balloons

Hot-air balloons float in the sky.
They go up, up, and away!

basket | burner

Helicopters

Helicopters whir through the air. Their blades spin around.

blade

Boats

Boats glide on the water.
They float over
the waves.

bow

Spacecraft

Space shuttles and rockets zoom off into space. Blast off!

orbiter

launch pad

Glossary

bicycle
a vehicle with two wheels

bus
a road vehicle that travels along a fixed route

helicopter
an aircraft with spinning blades

space shuttle
a flying vehicle that travels into space and back again

tractor
a four-wheeled farm vehicle

Index

air   24

airplanes   20

bicycles 16

boats   26

buses   18

cars   8

farms   14

fields 14

helicopters   24

highway   10

hot-air balloons   22

paths   16

railroad tracks   12

roads   8

rockets   28

sky   20, 22

space   28

space shuttles   28

spacecraft   28

streets   18

tractors   14

trains   12

trucks   10

water   26

Quiz

Answer the questions to see what you have learned. Check your answers with an adult.

1. What do trucks carry in their trailers?
2. Where can you find a tractor?
3. What does an airplane use to fly?
4. What are two things that can go into space?
5. Draw a picture of your favorite way to travel.

1. Heavy loads 2. On a farm 3. Its wings and engines
4. Space shuttles and rockets 5. Answers will vary